ADHD MANAGEMENT FOR OLDER WOMEN

Navigating symptoms and treatment options in adulthood

Medius Dawson

Copyright © 2022 Medius Dawson.

The information contained in this book has been compiled from sources believed to be reliable and accurate. The publisher, however, makes no warranty, express or implied, with respect to the material contained herein.

The information in this book is intended to serve as general guidance and should not be used as a substitute for professional medical advice. It is not intended to diagnose, treat, cure, or prevent any disease or medical condition. It is always best to consult a qualified medical professional with any questions or concerns you may have regarding a medical condition.

The publisher shall not be liable for any loss, damage, or injury caused by reliance upon any information contained in this book

Table of contents

CHAPTER I

Introduction

A. Overview of ADHD in older women:

Attention-deficit/hyperactivity disorder (ADHD) is a neurodevelopmental condition that affects both children and adults. While it is more usually linked with children, it may also afflict older women. According to the National Resource Center on ADHD, an estimated 4% of adults have ADHD. However, the prevalence of ADHD in older women is not well-documented and may be underdiagnosed.

ADHD is characterized by symptoms such as trouble concentration, impulsivity, and hyperactivity. These symptoms can have a major influence on an individual's capacity to function in numerous parts of their life, such as job, education, and relationships. In older women, symptoms may be different than those found in children or younger people, and may be misinterpreted for other diseases such as sadness, anxiety, or menopause-related symptoms.

The origins of ADHD are not well-understood, however it is considered to be connected to a mix of genetic, environmental, and developmental factors.

Risk factors for ADHD in older women include a family history of the illness, exposure to environmental pollutants, and specific prenatal disorders.

Proper diagnosis and management of ADHD in older women is critical for enhancing their overall well-being. This comprises a complete examination that takes into consideration the individual's medical history, symptoms, and functional impairment, as well as the use of medicines, behavioral therapy, and lifestyle modifications to manage symptoms.

B.   Importance   of   proper management:

Proper management of ADHD in older women is crucial to enhancing their overall quality of life. Without adequate management, symptoms of ADHD can have a substantial influence on an individual's ability to perform in numerous parts of their life, such as job, education, and relationships.

Proper care entails a complete examination that takes into consideration the individual's medical history, symptoms, and functional impairment. This examination can assist to rule out any underlying illnesses that may be contributing to symptoms and ensure that the accurate diagnosis is established.

There are numerous treatment options available for ADHD in older women, including medicines, behavioral therapy, and lifestyle modifications. Drugs, such as stimulant and non-stimulant medications can assist to treat symptoms such as difficulties concentration and impulsivity. Behavioral treatment, such as cognitive-behavioral therapy and mindfulness-based therapy, can help patients learn new techniques to manage their symptoms and enhance their quality of life. Lifestyle adjustments, such as exercise, food and nutrition, and sleep management, can also have a good influence on controlling symptoms of ADHD.

Additionally, many older women with ADHD also suffer from comorbid illnesses such as depression, anxiety, and drug misuse, which can influence the efficiency of therapy for ADHD. Proper care of these disorders is vital for enhancing overall well-being.

In summary, correct management of ADHD in older women is critical for improving their overall quality of life and addressing the impact of symptoms on many parts of their life, and for managing comorbid illnesses that can impair the effectiveness of therapy for ADHD.

CHAPTER II

Symptoms of ADHD in older women

A. Common symptoms

The common symptoms of ADHD in older women are comparable to those encountered in children and younger people. These include:

- Difficulty focusing: Individuals with ADHD may have a hard time paying attention and may become easily distracted. They may also have difficulty completing tasks that require sustained attention.

- Impulsivity: Individuals with ADHD may act impulsively without thinking about the consequences of their actions. They may also have problems waiting their time or interrupting others.

- Hyperactivity: Some persons with ADHD may experience signs of hyperactivity, such as fidgeting, wriggling, and feeling restless.

- Disorganization: Individuals with ADHD may have difficulties organizing their thoughts and tasks, and may struggle to keep track of their possessions or appointments.

- Memory issues: Individuals with ADHD may have trouble recalling new knowledge and have problems with working memory.

- Emotional instability: Individuals with ADHD may have difficulties managing their emotions and may be prone to outbursts of rage or irritation.

It's crucial to note that these symptoms might vary from person to person and may not be present in all older women with ADHD. Additionally, older women with ADHD may suffer certain symptoms that are distinct from those found in children or younger adults, for example, they may have less hyperactivity and more impulsivity, or issues with time management, organization, and planning.

B. How symptoms may differ from those in younger individuals

In older women, symptoms of ADHD may differ from those experienced in children or younger people. Some possible variations include:

- Less hyperactivity: Hyperactivity is frequently viewed as a primary sign of ADHD in youngsters, although it may be less apparent or nonexistent in older women.

- More impulsivity: Impulsivity may be more prominent in older women with ADHD, since they may have difficulties managing their impulses and acting on them without thinking.

- More challenges with time management and organization: Older women with ADHD may have more difficulty with time management and organization since they have more duties and demands in their everyday life.

- Greater challenges with planning and decision making: Older women with ADHD may have more difficulty with planning and decision making, which can impede their ability to operate in numerous parts of their lives.

- Greater issues with memory: Older women with ADHD may have more problems with memory, which can limit their ability to operate in numerous parts of their lives.

- More emotional instability: Older women with ADHD may have more emotional instability, which can impede their ability to function in numerous facets of their lives.

It's crucial to note that these variances may vary from person to person and not all older women with ADHD will experience all of these abnormalities. A detailed examination and appropriate diagnosis is crucial to ascertain the precise symptoms and how they influence the individual's everyday life.

C. Impact of symptoms on daily life

The symptoms of ADHD can have a substantial influence on the everyday life of older women. Some of the ways in which symptoms might disrupt daily living include:

- Trouble at work: Older women with ADHD may have problems finishing tasks and keeping focused on their jobs, which can lead to poor job performance and difficulty rising in their professions.
- Trouble in academic settings: Older women with ADHD may have difficulty completing tasks and remaining focused in academic settings, which can limit their ability to succeed in school.
- Issues in relationships: Older women with ADHD may have problems maintaining relationships owing to impulsivity, poor communication skills, and difficulty managing emotions.

- Challenges with organization and time management: Older women with ADHD may have difficulty keeping track of appointments, managing their time, and remaining organized, which can lead to challenges with meeting deadlines and finishing assignments.

- Difficulties with self-esteem: Older women with ADHD may have difficulty with self-esteem, feeling that they are not capable or clever enough, or feeling overwhelmed by the challenges of their everyday life.

It's crucial to note that these challenges might vary from person to person, and not all older women with ADHD will suffer all of these difficulties. However, these symptoms can have a considerable influence on an older woman's capacity to perform in numerous facets of their life, which is why correct management is crucial to enhance their overall quality of life.

CHAPTER III

Diagnosis and assessment

A. How ADHD is diagnosed in older women

ADHD is diagnosed in older women using the same criteria as in children and younger people. The Diagnostic and Statistical Manual of Mental Disorders (DSM-5) is the main instrument used by healthcare practitioners to diagnose ADHD. The requirements include:

- Inattention: Six or more symptoms of inattention for at least six months, which include difficulties paying attention, trouble following through on tasks, and problems with organizing.

- Hyperactivity-impulsivity: Six or more symptoms of hyperactivity-impulsivity for at least six months, which include fidgeting, trouble sitting still, and behaving impulsively without thinking.

- Symptoms that produce impairment: The symptoms must cause considerable impairment in two or more aspects of an individual's life, such as school, work, or relationships.

- Symptoms that are not better described by another illness: The symptoms must not be better explained by another condition, such as depression, anxiety, or a sleep problem.

It's crucial to highlight that the diagnosis of ADHD in older women can be hard, as symptoms may differ from those found in children or younger people, and may be confused for other disorders. A complete examination that takes into considerations the individual's medical history, symptoms, and functional impairment is crucial to establish an appropriate diagnosis.

Additionally, healthcare practitioners may utilize rating scales, questionnaires, and interviews to evaluate symptoms, these tools can assist to obtain additional information about the individual's symptoms, how they influence their daily life, and how severe they are.

It's also crucial to highlight that a diagnosis of ADHD in older women should be made by a trained healthcare practitioner, such as a psychiatrist, psychologist, or neurologist with experience in the diagnosis and treatment of ADHD.

B. Importance of a comprehensive assessment

A complete examination is a critical step in the diagnosis and management of ADHD in older women. It helps to ensure that the accurate diagnosis is established and that all relevant aspects are taken into account when formulating a treatment plan.

A full examination often includes:

- Medical history: The healthcare professional will take a full medical history, including any past or present medical issues, medicines, and family history of ADHD or other mental health conditions.

- Symptom assessment: The healthcare professional will utilize rating scales, questionnaires, and interviews to evaluate symptoms, gather additional information about the individual's symptoms, how they influence their daily life, and how severe they are.

- Functional impairment assessment: The healthcare expert will evaluate how the symptoms influence the individual's ability to function in many parts of their life, such as job, school, and relationships.

- Differential diagnosis: The healthcare expert will explore alternative diagnoses, such as depression, anxiety, or other diseases that may be contributing to symptoms and rule them out before reaching a conclusive diagnosis of ADHD.

This complete review is necessary for various reasons:

- It helps to guarantee an accurate diagnosis: A complete examination takes into consideration all relevant aspects, which can assist to ensure an accurate diagnosis of ADHD.

- It helps to detect comorbid conditions: A full evaluation can help to uncover any comorbid conditions, such as depression, anxiety, or drug misuse that may be impacting the individual's symptoms and general well-being.

- It helps to develop an effective treatment plan: A comprehensive assessment provides a detailed understanding of the individual's symptoms, how they affect their daily life, and how severe they are, which can help to develop an effective treatment plan that addresses the individual's specific needs.

- It helps to evaluate the effectiveness of therapy: A complete evaluation may be used to evaluate the effectiveness of treatment over time by monitoring the individual's symptoms and functional impairment.

In summary, a complete examination is a critical step in the diagnosis and management of ADHD in older women. It helps to establish an accurate diagnosis, identify comorbid diseases, and design an effective treatment plan that fits the individual's particular requirements. Regular follow-up exams can also assist to evaluate the effectiveness of therapy over time and make appropriate modifications. It is crucial that the examination is done by a skilled healthcare practitioner with experience in the diagnosis and treatment of ADHD.

C. Differential diagnosis

Differential diagnosis is the process of identifying a certain ailment from others that may have similar symptoms.
It is a critical step in the diagnosis of ADHD in older women, since symptoms may be misinterpreted for other illnesses.

Some disorders that may be explored during the differential diagnosis of ADHD in older women include:

- Depression: Older women with ADHD may also exhibit signs of depression, such as poor mood, loss of interest in activities, and difficulties focusing.
- Anxiety: Older women with ADHD may also exhibit signs of anxiety, such as worry, restlessness, and difficulty sleeping.
- Menopause-related symptoms: Older women with ADHD may experience symptoms that overlap with menopause-related symptoms, such as hot flashes, irritability, and problems sleeping.
- Sleep problems: Older women with ADHD may have symptoms that overlap with sleep disorders, such as insomnia, sleep apnea, and restless leg syndrome.
- Drug abuse: Older women with ADHD may be at risk for substance addiction, which can damage their ability to focus and make decisions.

It's crucial to remember that these diseases can co-occur with ADHD and may impair the individual's symptoms and general well-being.

A complete examination that takes into considerations the individual's medical history, symptoms, and functional impairment can assist to rule out other underlying illnesses and assure an accurate diagnosis of ADHD.

Additionally, it's crucial to realize that various disorders may have varied treatment choices; consequently, a proper diagnosis will guarantee that the client receives the best therapy for their unique ailment.

CHAPTER IV

Treatment options

A. Medications:

Medications such as stimulants and non-stimulants can be effective in improving symptoms of ADHD.

1. Stimulant medications:

Stimulant drugs, such as Ritalin, Adderall, and Concerta, act by boosting the levels of specific neurotransmitters in the brain, such as dopamine and norepinephrine, which can enhance attention and impulse control. These drugs are normally given once or twice a day and their effects often persist for many hours. However, they may have certain negative effects such as sleeplessness, reduced appetite, and headaches.

2. Non-stimulant medications:

Non-stimulant drugs, such as Strattera and Intuniv, act by changing the levels of other neurotransmitters in the brain, such as norepinephrine, and can also be useful in alleviating symptoms. These drugs are normally given once a day and their effects typically last for 24 hours. They also may have some adverse effects such as sleepiness, nausea, and stomach pain.

It's crucial to remember that older women may have varying reactions to these drugs and it may take some time to locate the proper prescription at the optimum dosage. Medications should be provided and managed by a skilled healthcare provider with experience in the treatment of ADHD.

B. Behavioral therapy

Behavioral treatment: Behavioral therapy, such as cognitive-behavioral therapy and mindfulness-based therapy, can help older women with ADHD learn new ways to control their symptoms and enhance their quality of life. Behavioral treatment can assist persons with ADHD acquire skills such as time management, organization, and impulse control, it can also help to address any emotional challenges that may come as a result of the illness. Behavioral therapy is generally delivered by a qualified therapist or counselor and can be done alone or in a group setting.

1. Cognitive-behavioral therapy

Cognitive-behavioral therapy (CBT) is a form of behavioral treatment that can be beneficial in treating ADHD in older women. CBT is a sort of talk therapy that focuses on the link between an individual's ideas, feelings, and behaviors.

During CBT, the therapist works with the person to identify and alter negative thinking patterns and beliefs that may be contributing to their symptoms.
The therapist may also teach the person new coping methods and skills to control their symptoms.

Cognitive-behavioral treatment can benefit older women with ADHD in the following ways:

- Time management: CBT can help persons with ADHD acquire skills such as time management, organization, and impulse control.

- Problem-solving: CBT can enable persons with ADHD to build problem-solving abilities to manage their symptoms more successfully.

- Addressing negative ideas: CBT can help persons with ADHD to confront unpleasant thoughts and feelings that may be causing discomfort, and encouraging them to establish new, more optimistic views.

- Addressing emotional challenges: CBT can help persons with ADHD to handle any emotional difficulties that may occur as a result of the disorder, such as poor self-esteem, sadness, or anxiety.

CBT is generally delivered by a certified therapist or counselor and can be done alone or in a group setting.

It's important to remember that CBT may not be helpful for everyone, and it may take some time to discover the proper therapist and treatment plan that works best for the person.

Additionally, it's also crucial to remember that CBT should be used in conjunction with other treatment choices, including as medication and lifestyle modifications, to receive the greatest outcomes.

2. Mindfulness-based therapy

Mindfulness-based treatment is a sort of behavioral therapy that can be useful in treating ADHD in older women. Mindfulness-based therapy is a style of treatment that stresses the practice of mindfulness, which is the act of paying attention to the present moment in a non-judgmental way.

During mindfulness-based treatment, the therapist will teach the individual mindfulness skills, such as meditation, yoga, and deep breathing, to encourage them to concentrate their attention on the present now and improve their symptoms.

Mindfulness-based treatment can assist older women with ADHD in the following ways:

- Improving attention and concentration: Mindfulness practices can help persons with ADHD to improve their attention and focus, which can help to minimize symptoms of ADHD.

- Managing impulsivity: Mindfulness practices can help persons with ADHD to control impulsivity by encouraging them to pause and analyze their actions before acting.

- Managing emotions: Mindfulness practices can help persons with ADHD to regulate emotions by helping them to observe and understand their feelings rather than being governed by them.

- Improving self-esteem: Mindfulness practices can help persons with ADHD to enhance self-esteem by training them to accept themselves as they are and not criticize themselves for their symptoms.

Mindfulness-based therapy is generally delivered by a qualified therapist or counselor and can be done individually or in a group setting. It's important to note that mindfulness-based therapy may not be beneficial for everyone, and it may take some time to discover the ideal therapist and treatment plan that works best for the person.

Additionally, it's also crucial to remember that mindfulness-based therapy should be used in conjunction with other treatment choices, including as medication and lifestyle modifications, to receive the greatest outcomes.

c. Lifestyle changes

Lifestyle adjustments, such as exercise, food, and sleep management, can also have a good influence on treating symptoms of ADHD. Regular physical activity can assist improve attention, focus, and self-control, a well-balanced diet rich in fruits, vegetables, and lean protein can help improve symptoms, and proper sleep can help those with ADHD better manage their symptoms.

1. Exercise

Exercise can be a helpful therapeutic choice for treating symptoms of ADHD in older women. Regular physical activity has been demonstrated to improve cognitive performance, lessen symptoms of ADHD, and increase general well-being.

The benefits of exercise for those with ADHD include:

- Improving attention and focus: Exercise can assist to enhance blood flow to the brain, which can improve cognitive performance and minimize symptoms of ADHD.
- Reducing hyperactivity: Exercise can assist to lessen hyperactivity by giving an outlet for extra energy.
- Improving mood: Exercise can produce endorphins, which are chemicals in the brain that can boost mood and lessen symptoms of melancholy and anxiety.
- Improving sleep: Exercise can assist to improve sleep quality, which can enable persons with ADHD to manage their symptoms more successfully.

It's crucial to remember that exercise should be done under the advice of a certified healthcare expert to ensure that it is safe and beneficial for the individual.

A customized workout plan that takes into consideration the individual's particular demands and talents is the best method to ensure that the individual will be able to remain with the fitness program in the long run.

It's also crucial to remember that exercise should be done in conjunction with other treatment choices, such as medicine and therapy, to receive the greatest outcomes.

2. Diet and nutrition

Diet and nutrition can play a significant role in treating symptoms of ADHD in older women.
A well-balanced diet that is rich in fruits, vegetables, and lean protein will help to offer the required nutrients for normal brain function and can assist to boost mood and energy levels.

Some dietary adjustments that might be advantageous for persons with ADHD include:

- Eating a well-balanced diet: A well-balanced diet that is rich in fruits, vegetables, and lean protein will help to give the required nutrients for normal brain function and can help to boost mood and energy levels.
- Eating at regular intervals: Eating at regular intervals throughout the day can assist to maintain stable blood sugar levels, which can aid to increase focus and attention.
- Avoiding processed foods: Processed foods can be heavy in sugar, artificial colors, and preservatives, which can impact mood and behavior.

- Avoiding caffeine: Coffee can impair sleep and can increase symptoms of ADHD, thus it is suggested to restrict or avoid caffeine.

It's crucial to remember that diet and nutrition should be utilized in conjunction with other treatment choices, such as medicine and therapy, to obtain the greatest outcomes. A licensed dietitian with experience in ADHD might be consulted to give help on a customized food plan.

It's also important to remember that dietary modifications may not be successful for everyone and it's not a substitute for other therapies, but can be a supportive tool to help manage the symptoms of ADHD.

3. Sleep management

Sleep management can be an essential element of controlling symptoms of ADHD in older women. Adequate sleep is vital for general well-being, and can assist to increase focus and attentiveness during the day. However, persons with ADHD may have difficulties going asleep or staying asleep, which can worsen symptoms.

Some options for enhancing sleep for persons with ADHD include:

- Establishing a regular sleep schedule: Going to bed and getting up at the same time every day can assist to regulate the body's internal clock and enhance sleep quality.
- Creating a calming night ritual: Establishing a relaxing bedtime habit, such as reading a book

or taking a warm bath, can assist to signal to the body that it is time to sleep.

- Creating a good sleep environment: Creating a comfortable sleep environment, such as keeping the room dark, quiet, and at a suitable temperature, can assist to enhance sleep quality.
- Avoiding stimulating activities before bedtime: Avoiding stimulating activities, such as watching TV or using a computer, before bedtime can assist to enhance sleep quality.
- Avoiding coffee and nicotine before night: Caffeine and nicotine are stimulants that can influence sleep, thus it is suggested to avoid ingesting these drugs before bedtime.

It's crucial to remember that sleep management should be used in conjunction with other treatment choices, such as medicine and therapy, to obtain the greatest outcomes.

It's also crucial to remember that persons with ADHD may have additional sleep problems such as insomnia, sleep apnea and restless leg syndrome; therefore, it is vital to speak with a skilled healthcare practitioner to rule out any other underlying illness.

CHAPTER V

Managing comorbid conditions

Managing comorbid diseases is a crucial element of treating ADHD in older women, since many older women with ADHD also suffer from other illnesses such as depression, anxiety, and drug addiction. These disorders can interact with and impact the symptoms of ADHD, and their care should be done in collaboration with the management of ADHD.

Some ways for addressing comorbid conditions include:

- Meds: Medications such as antidepressants and anti-anxiety medications can be beneficial in treating comorbid illnesses such as depression and anxiety.
- Behavioral treatment: Behavioral therapies such as cognitive-behavioral therapy and mindfulness-based therapy can be useful in treating comorbid problems such as depression and anxiety.
- Substance abuse therapy: Substance abuse treatment can be beneficial in treating comorbid disorders such as substance misuse.
- Coordination of care: Coordination of treatment amongst healthcare experts such as primary care physician, psychiatrist, and therapist can be useful in managing comorbid disorders.

It's crucial to remember that comorbid disorders may have different treatment choices; therefore, a correct diagnosis is important to ensure that the client receives the best therapy for their unique ailment.

Additionally, it's vital to highlight that comorbid disorders should be addressed in collaboration with the therapy of ADHD, to ensure that the individual receives thorough and successful treatment.

A. Depression and anxiety

Depression and anxiety are frequent comorbid illnesses that can emerge in older women with ADHD. These disorders can interact with and impact the symptoms of ADHD, and their care should be done in collaboration with the management of ADHD.

Depression is a frequent mood condition that is characterized by feelings of sorrow, despair, and a loss of interest in activities. It can impede a person's capacity to operate in their everyday life. Symptoms of depression may include feelings of melancholy, despair, guilt, and a loss of interest in activities.

Anxiety is a frequent disorder characterized by emotions of concern, uneasiness, and dread. It can impede a person's capacity to operate in their everyday life. Symptoms of anxiety may include excessive concern, anxiousness, and terror.

Some ways for addressing sadness and anxiety include:

- Meds: Medications such as antidepressants and anti-anxiety medications can be beneficial in treating depression and anxiety.
- Behavioral treatment: Behavioral therapies such as cognitive-behavioral therapy and mindfulness-based therapy can be useful in treating depression and anxiety.
- Lifestyle adjustments: Lifestyle improvements such as exercise, nutrition, and sleep management can be useful in controlling depression and anxiety.

It's crucial to remember that depression and anxiety are complicated disorders that may have multiple treatment choices; therefore, a correct diagnosis is important to guarantee that the individual receives the best treatment for their unique condition. Additionally, it's vital to highlight that depression and anxiety should be addressed in collaboration with the therapy of ADHD, to ensure that the individual receives thorough and successful treatment.

B. Substance abuse

Substance misuse is a frequent comorbid disease that can emerge in older women with ADHD. Substance abuse is the excessive use of drugs or alcohol, which can have detrimental impacts on an individual's physical and mental health, relationships, and daily life.

Individuals with ADHD may be at a higher risk for substance misuse, since they may use substances to cope with symptoms or to increase their concentration and attention. Substance usage can also increase symptoms of ADHD and make it more difficult to control the illness.

Some ways for addressing drug misuse include:

- Substance abuse therapy: Substance abuse treatment programs, such as detoxification, rehabilitation, and counseling, can be beneficial in treating substance misuse.

- Medications: Medications such as naltrexone and acamprosate can be beneficial in controlling substance dependence.

- Behavioral treatment: Behavioral therapies such as cognitive-behavioral therapy and mindfulness-based therapy can be useful in controlling drug misuse.

It's crucial to remember that drug abuse is a complicated disorder that may have multiple treatment choices; therefore, a correct diagnosis is important to guarantee that the individual receives the right therapy for their unique problem.

Additionally, it's vital to highlight that drug misuse should be addressed in collaboration with the management of ADHD, to ensure that the individual receives thorough and successful therapy.

C. Other conditions commonly seen in older women with ADHD

Other issues that are typically encountered in older women with ADHD include:

- Menopause: Menopause is a normal biological process that happens in women as they age, defined by the end of menstrual cycles. It can induce symptoms such as hot flashes, nocturnal sweats, and sleep difficulties. These symptoms can increase symptoms of ADHD and make it more difficult to control the illness.

- Cardiovascular disease: Cardiovascular disease is a set of disorders that affect the heart and blood arteries. It can produce symptoms such as chest discomfort, shortness of breath, and exhaustion. These symptoms can increase symptoms of ADHD and make it more difficult to control the illness.

- Thyroid problems: Thyroid disorders are ailments that affect the thyroid gland, which is a tiny gland found in the neck that produces hormones that regulate metabolism. Thyroid issues can produce symptoms such as weight gain, exhaustion, and irritability. These symptoms can increase symptoms of ADHD and make it more difficult to control the illness.

- Chronic pain: Chronic pain is pain that lasts for more than three months. It can produce symptoms such as headaches, back discomfort, and muscular soreness. These symptoms can increase symptoms of ADHD and make it more difficult to control the illness.

It's essential to note that various disorders may have varied treatment choices; therefore, a proper diagnosis is important to ensure that the client receives the best therapy for their unique ailment. Additionally, it's vital to emphasize that these illnesses should be addressed in collaboration with the management of ADHD, to ensure that the individual receives thorough and successful therapy.

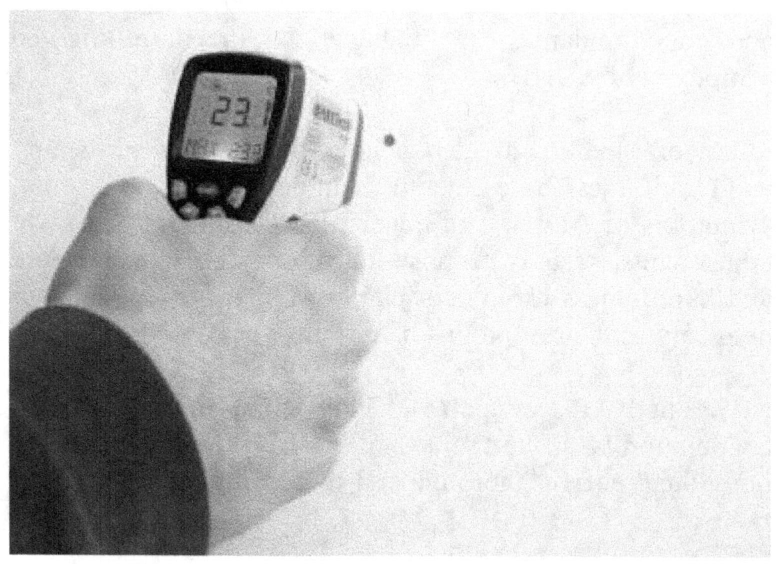

CHAPTER VI

Conclusion

A. Summary of key points

ADHD care for older women is significant as ADHD symptoms can linger into adulthood and can have a severe influence on everyday living. Proper management of ADHD in older women includes a full examination and ongoing follow-up care with a skilled healthcare expert.

Treatment options for ADHD in older women include medicines, behavioral therapy, lifestyle modifications and management of comorbid diseases such as depression, anxiety and drug misuse. Medications, such as stimulants and non-stimulants, can be beneficial in controlling the symptoms of ADHD.

Behavioral treatment, such as cognitive-behavioral therapy and mindfulness-based therapy, can be useful in controlling symptoms of ADHD and concomitant disorders. Lifestyle adjustments, such as exercise, nutrition, sleep management and mindfulness techniques can be supportive strategies to help control the symptoms of ADHD.

Additionally, it's crucial to handle comorbid illnesses in cooperation with the therapy of ADHD to ensure that the individual receives thorough and successful treatment.

Other problems such as menopause, cardiovascular disease, thyroid disorders, and chronic pain are typically encountered in older women with ADHD and should also be taken into mind while addressing the illness.

It is crucial to note that ADHD management is a continuous process and requires frequent follow-up care with a skilled healthcare expert. This may involve frequent check-ins with a primary care physician, psychiatrist or a therapist. Medicine management is a crucial aspect of the treatment and may involve regular modifications to the amount or kind of medication administered. Behavioral therapy and lifestyle adjustments are also significant components of ADHD management and may need regular meetings with a therapist or counselor.

It is also vital to engage family members and caregivers in the treatment process, as they may provide support and aid with controlling symptoms. This includes aiding with medication administration, offering emotional support, and helping with lifestyle modifications such as exercise and food.

It's crucial to be patient with the management process since it may take time to discover the correct treatment plan that works for the person. It's also crucial to be open-minded about exploring new treatment approaches and to not hesitate to seek expert aid if needed.

In conclusion, ADHD management for older women is an essential procedure that demands a thorough strategy. Medication, behavioral therapy, lifestyle modifications, and care of concomitant diseases are all key components of the process.

Regular follow-up consultations with a skilled healthcare practitioner, as well as the engagement of family members and caregivers are critical for controlling symptoms and increasing overall well-being.

B. Resources for further information and support:

There are several resources available for more information and assistance for older women with ADHD. These include:

- National Institute of Mental Health (NIMH): The NIMH is a federal agency that offers information on mental health diseases, including ADHD. They give information on the causes, symptoms, and treatment of ADHD, as well as resources for support and research.

- American Psychiatric Association (APA): The APA is the premier professional organization for psychiatrists in the United States. They give information about mental health issues, including ADHD, as well as resources for assistance and research.

- American Psychological Association (APA): The APA is the premier professional organization for psychologists in the United States.

- They give information about mental health issues, including ADHD, as well as resources for assistance and research.

- ADHD Women's Palooza: This is a convention for women with ADHD, which includes courses and support groups for persons with ADHD and their families.

- Attention Deficit Disorder Association (ADDA): The ADDA is a non-profit organization that provides information and support for persons with ADHD and their families. They give information on the causes, symptoms, and treatment of ADHD, as well as resources for support and research.

- CHADD (Children and Adults with Attention-Deficit/Hyperactivity Disorder): CHADD is a non-profit organization that provides information and support for persons with ADHD and their families. They give information on the causes, symptoms, and treatment of ADHD, as well as resources for support and research.

- Online support groups: There are several online support groups for persons with ADHD and their families. These communities give a venue for individuals to share their stories, ask questions, and provide support to one another.

It's crucial to remember that these materials are not a substitute for expert medical advice and diagnosis and individuals should contact with a competent healthcare practitioner for individualized treatment and assistance.

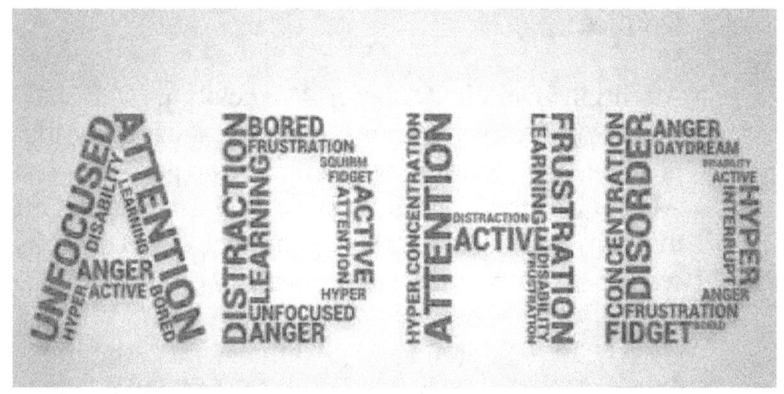